THE OFFICIAL
MANCHESTER
UNITED
ANNUAL 2006

ADAM BOSTOCK & BEN HIBBS

First Published in 2005

Copyright © 2005
Manchester United Plc
Text and design copyright ©
2005 Carlton Publishing Group

Manufactured and distributed by
Carlton Publishing Group
20 Mortimer Street
London W1T 3JW

A CIP catalogue for this book is available from the
British Library.

ISBN 0 233 00120 4

Managing Editor: **Martin Corteel**
Project Art Editor: **Luke Griffin**
Design and Editorial: **Andy Jones, Deborah Martin**
Photography: **John Peters, Matthew Peters and
Tom Purslow for Manchester United FC**
Picture Research: **Tom Wright**
Production: **Lisa French**

Printed in Italy

Fans can purchase most of the photos in this book
from: www.manutdpics.com

Contents

Millennium Milestone: Fergie's 1000 Games	4
League Review 2004/05	6
The Total Footballer: Rooney	16
The Front Men: Saha, Smith, Van Nistelrooy	18
United's Quiet Man: Scholes	20
Midfield Maestros: Fletcher, Keane, Miller	22
Cup Quests 2004/05	24
FA Cup Final/Reserves Win the Quadruple!	26
The Entertainer: Ronaldo	28
Touchline Troops: Bellion, Giggs, Fortune	30
Champions League Review	32
Who Am I? Puzzle	34
Can You Do An Ole? Puzzle and Profile	36
Backbone Boys: Ferdinand, Howard	38
Fergie's Flexible Defenders: Brown, O'Shea, Silvestre	40
Ones to Watch: United Stars of the Future?	42
Wayne's World: Photo-story	44
Formidable Full-backs: Neville, Heinze and Neville	46
Design Your Own Away Kit	48
Behind the Scenes: Manchester to Milan	50
The Best Of Enemies	52
Can You Clinch the Premiership? Quiz	54
Commentary Quiz	56
Fred the Red	58
Answers to Puzzles	60

Millennium Milestone

Five Games That Define Fergie's Reign

In November 2004, **Sir Alex Ferguson** celebrated 1000 games in charge of Manchester United with a 2–1 Champions League victory over Olympique Lyonnais at Old Trafford.

The Reds' boss proudly led out his team, now ranked as one of the most powerful forces in European football. But it was a far cry from his very first game in charge, against Oxford United in November 1986.

We've picked five games from Ferguson's first 1000 that symbolise his time at the club and tell the story of United's rise and rise during his managerial reign…

Oxford United 2–0 Manchester United
Football League Division One
Manor Ground, Oxford,
7 November 1986

Ferguson arrived from Aberdeen with United languishing in 18th spot in Division One, an injury crisis denying him the services of Bryan Robson, Norman Whiteside, Gordan Strachan and John Sivebaek for this trip. In the 13 League games up to the Scot's arrival, United had won just three and lost six. Fan frustration was amplified as the Reds from Manchester had failed to break the domination of their North-west neighbours, the Reds from Liverpool. United lost 2–0 in Ferguson's opening game against Oxford, bleakly spelling out the mammoth task that lay ahead.

Fergie's view: "I remember sitting on the plane on my way back to Aberdeen that evening, thinking: 'I've got a really hard job on my hands.' After that game, myself and the staff set about building a football club, not a football team."

Port Vale 1–2 Manchester United
League Cup Second Round 1st Leg
Vale Park, Stoke-on-Trent,
21 September 1994
Scorer: Scholes (2)

There are numerous matches of greater incident in more glamorous locations than this League Cup tie in Stoke-on-Trent. However, this game is recognised as the birth of one of the most crucial components of Ferguson's reign: the emergence of United's youth. Promising talents like Scholes, Neville, Beckham and Butt among others were given a rare chance of first-team football. First-team players were rested, with much discussion, most notably in the Houses of Parliament where Ferguson's selection policy was debated. Vale fans hoping to see United's Double-winning side bombarded radio phone-ins, while football's authorities pondered disciplinary action. But the young players that night would form the nucleus of one the most formidable teams in English football history. United went 1–0 down after seven minutes against Vale, but two goals from debutant Paul Scholes – a deft finish and a header – secured a memorable victory.

Fergie's view: "I always remember the local MP for Stoke complaining about us playing a weakened team! We got off to a bad start but we just kept playing football and eventually came good."

1000 games as United boss

Fergie's 1000 Games: The Breakdown

Competition	P	W	D	L	F	A
Premiership	482	298	113	71	943	439
Division One	225	97	70	58	319	227
FA Cup	78	53	14	11	149	64
League Cup	65	41	7	17	112	69
Community Shield	11	2	4	5	13	16
Champions League	116	62	31	23	219	113
Cup Winners' Cup	13	8	4	1	20	8
UEFA Cup	4	0	4	0	2	2
European Super Cup	2	1	0	1	1	1
Intercontinental Championship	1	1	0	0	1	0
World Club Championship	3	1	1	1	4	4
Total	1000	564	248	188	1783	943

Arsenal 1–2 Manchester United
FA Cup Semi-Final Replay
Villa Park, Birmingham, 14 April 1999
Scorers: Beckham, Giggs

The Treble-winning season, and in particular the final few months of the campaign, will forever be remembered as the most exhilarating and definitive period in Sir Alex's managerial career. United had drawn four of their last five games – including the first-leg European Cup semi-final with Juventus – going into this FA Cup semi-final replay against Arsenal. A more dramatic FA Cup semi-final you are not likely to find. The first attempt ended 0–0 and forced a replay. David Beckham put United in the lead before Bergkamp drew Arsenal level on 69 minutes. Step forward Ryan Giggs in extra time. The Welshman's remarkable solo winner in the 109th minute proved the critical difference between two teams that had been practically inseparable for 199 minutes.

Fergie's view: "Winning that game was crucial to getting the Treble; it galvanised everyone by getting us to our first final."

Juventus 2–3 Manchester United
European Cup Semi-Final 2nd Leg
Stadio delle Alpi, Turin, 21 April 1999
Scorers: Keane, Yorke, Cole

Football at the very highest level encompasses great skill, guile, flair and technique. But one of the most underestimated assets of great players, teams and managers is character. There can be few greater examples of a team's and its manager's personalities coming to the fore as this match in Turin. 0–2 down following two Filippo Inzaghi goals in the opening ten minutes and United were staring at a gut-wrenching European Cup exit. But Keane's header after 24 minutes and his utterly selfless and defiant display, despite picking up a yellow card that would make him miss the final through suspension, summed up the spirit in the team. From then, Yorke and Cole grabbed a goal apiece and sent United on the road to a glorious Treble.

Fergie's view: "Without question, our phenomenal performance against Juventus in Turin was the best we've ever had. Everyone did their bit – there were no failures on that night."

Manchester United 2–1 Bayern Munich
European Cup Final
Nou Camp, Barcelona, 26 May 1999
Scorers: Sheringham, Solskjaer

If the semi-final display against Juventus bordered on perfection, the final could not be matched for its drama. Mario Basler's free-kick put Bayern in front after just six minutes, while Mehmet Scholl and Carsten Jancker both hit the woodwork in the second half. The trophy United craved was drifting despairingly out of reach. But the all-important equaliser arrived from substitute Teddy Sheringham in injury time. Bayern cleared a corner only as far as Ryan Giggs. The Welshman scuffed his shot but Sheringham hooked the ball home. From then on European Cup success and an unprecedented Treble were a mere inevitability. In the dying moments, Sheringham flicked on Beckham's corner and Solskjaer's outstretched right boot put United 2–1 in front. Cue pandemonium among the players, staff and supporters. The historic victory fittingly occurred on 26 May, Sir Matt Busby's birthday.

Fergie's view: "When we were losing 1–0, I was thinking of what to say to my players. I was going to tell them they had been great all season; they had won a Double and got to the final of a European Cup and done everyone proud… that was all I could say. It was such a change in emotions just a few moments later."

LEAGUE REVIEW

Manchester United were thrown into the lions' den at the start of the Premiership race. The fixture computer forced the Reds to play their first league game away against Chelsea – runners-up in 2003/04 and one of the favourites for the title in 2004/05. Meanwhile, title-holders Arsenal were hoping to keep up an amazing run which had seen them go through the entire 2003/04 season without losing a single league game...

August 2004

If the task of winning their ninth Premiership title already seemed tough, then it was made a teeny bit tougher for United when they lost that opening game at Stamford Bridge, 0–1. Chelsea were hardly the better side, despite another summer influx of expensive new players. But they were rock-solid at the back, and accurate when it mattered in attack – Lampard scored the only goal from the penalty spot after Roy Keane was considered to have fouled Joe Cole.

The fixture computer was a bit kinder to United when it came to the second game – at home to the newly promoted Norwich City. But the Canaries were not easily knocked off their perch. To beat them 2–1, the Reds needed Alan Smith to score a superb volley on his Old Trafford debut. Otherwise, David Bellion's opening goal might have been worth only a point, with McVeigh scoring later for Norwich.

Smith raised his profile again in United's next away match. As a life-long Leeds supporter, Smith knew he'd have to work hard to win the affections of the United fans. Goals would certainly help his cause, especially if he scored them in the dying seconds. That's exactly what happened at Ewood Park where the Reds looked destined to lose 0–1. After conceding a goal to Dickov in the 18th minute, they found Blackburn's goalkeeper to be in frustratingly fine form. But Friedel's fortune finally ran out in injury time when Smith equalised. Phew!

Forty-eight hours later, United were in action again, hosting Everton in a Bank Holiday fixture. The home fans felt short-changed by the dull 0–0 draw but not for long. The club's money-men splashed the cash the following day, to sign – ironically – Everton's star player...

Chelsea 1–0 Man Utd
15-08-2004
Man Utd 2–1 Norwich City
21-08-2004 (Bellion, Smith)
Blackburn Rovers 1–1 Man Utd
28-08-2004 (Smith)
Man Utd 0–0 Everton
30-08-2004

September 2004

Wayne Rooney would have to wait a few weeks to play his first Premiership game for United. He arrived from Everton with the injury he suffered during Euro 2004, the tournament which had turned him into an England superstar. Fortunately, the Reds had another new-boy available to score his first goal in September.

Gabriel Heinze had also had a busy summer, winning a gold medal at the Athens Olympics with Argentina's soccer team. This delayed his United debut but it was worth the wait. Apart from giving the Reds a half-time lead at Bolton, he also put in a few crunching tackles, just

Above: **New boy Gabriel Heinze leaves Bolton's Okocha behind.**

Ruud van Nistelrooy reached a century of Premiership appearances by playing in the United v Liverpool match on 20 September 2004. He netted 68 league goals during those first 100 league games – a strike-rate that most players in the Premiership could only dream of.

Above: **Rio enjoys his return.**
Left: **Smith scores at Ewood.**
Right: **Sir Alex ends August by signing Everton's Wayne Rooney.**

what the doctor – or rather the Manager – ordered in a local derby!

When Nolan netted for the home side, it seemed United were heading for another draw. Worse still, Ferdinand – Les, not Rio – put Bolton 2–1 up with just two minutes left. Would Smith rescue the Reds with another last-gasp goal? Not this time but United were saved by the Bell-ion, David making it 2–2 with virtually the last kick of the game.

Frenchmen were flavour of the month in September. Nine days after Bellion's heroics at Bolton, Mikael Silvestre made his mark on the scoresheet with two goals against Liverpool – who were now coached by Rafael Benitez from Spain. Beating the old rivals 2–1 at Old Trafford was the perfect way to welcome back Rio Ferdinand, who played

Bolton Wanderers 2–2 Man Utd
11-09-2004 (Heinze, Bellion)
Man Utd 2–1 Liverpool
20-09-2004 (Silvestre 2)
Tottenham Hotspur 0–1 Man Utd
25-09-2004 (van Nistelrooy pen.)

his first game since January 2004 after being suspended.

United's next opponents were also under new management. Ex-France coach Jacques Santini had so far not lost a game as Spurs boss, but that was about to change! Ruud van Nistelrooy's first goal of the season – a first-half penalty – gave United their first away win.

October 2004

October is often a tricky time for Manchester United and so it proved again in 2004. However, the fans were treated to one great game – a storming 2–0 victory against Arsenal – before the month ended with a frightening performance at Fratton Park, the day before Hallowe'en!

Two dropped points at Old Trafford set the tone for a tough month in the Premiership. Missing several of their first-choice players, Middlesbrough seemed all-set for a thrashing. But Boro's young rookies were a force to be reckoned with, especially the left winger Downing, who drilled home the first goal in the first half. It remained 0–1 to the away team until United substitute Alan Smith produced his party-piece – the late equaliser – with only nine minutes left to go.

The goals were even harder to come by at Birmingham. Try as they might, United could not break down the Blues – not even with all four strikers on the field in the final half-hour. The 0–0 result gave Steve Bruce his first-ever point against Sir Alex Ferguson and left his old boss further behind Arsene Wenger's Arsenal in the title race.

The Reds were actually 11 points adrift of their arch-rivals as they kicked off against each other on the following

Above:**United fail to beat Middlesbrough at Old Trafford. L–R: Smith, Southgate, Gary Neville, Schwarzer, Cooper.**
Below: **Rooney celebrates his goal against Arsenal.**

Sunday. Arsenal were top of the table and still on top form, after winning or drawing the previous 49 games. An amazing record, but to United, it was also like a red rag to a bull! See our special feature on page 52 for details.

Sadly, the peak of beating Arsenal was followed by the trough of losing to Portsmouth – the south-coast side recorded their second win in a row over United, with goals by Unsworth (penalty) and Yakubu. Ronaldo rattled the post but no one in red could ripple the net on an afternoon we'd rather forget. Quick… let's read the next bit!

Wayne Rooney will never forget his 19th birthday. Born on 24 October 1985, he scored his first league goal for United on the same date in 2004, against Arsenal. The Gunners were also the victims of Wayne's first league goal for Everton in 2002… five days before his 17th birthday!

**Man Utd 1–1 Middlesborough 03-10-2004 (Smith)
Birmingham City 0–0 Man Utd 16-10-2004
Man Utd 2–0 Arsenal 24-10-2004 (van Nistelrooy pen., Rooney)
Portsmouth 2–0 Man Utd 30-10-2004**

Above: **Rooney puts the Reds on the road to victory at St James' Park by slotting the ball past Newcastle's Bramble and Given.**
Right: **Louis Saha is denied by City's David James.**
Below: **Ex-United star Nicky Butt tries to stop Ronaldo.**

November 2004

Sorry, reader… if you were looking for a quick recovery from the shock of losing to Portsmouth, then you've come to the wrong paragraph. United's goal supply dried up again in the first league game of November, against Manchester City of all people! Maybe the frustration was all too much for Alan Smith – he was sent off in the 89th minute after fouling Dunne, earlier he'd been booked for clashing with Bosvelt.

A trip to Tyneside turned out to be the tonic that United needed. In their best away performance of the season so far, the Reds rammed three goals into Newcastle's net. Rooney started and finished it, with strikes in the 7th and 90th minutes. Ruud scored the other from the spot in the 74th, three minutes after Shearer had raised the home fans' hopes with an equaliser.

Two of United's finest playmakers scored their first league goals of the season in the next match, at home to Charlton. Ryan Giggs grabbed his just before half-time, and Paul Scholes followed suit soon after, with a tremendous volley from Darren Fletcher's cross. Final score: 2–0.

The Reds carried their rediscovered form into the final league match of the month, away to West Brom. The Baggies had a new boss in the shape of former United captain Bryan Robson but, unlike another ex-skipper Steve Bruce, he could only keep his old club at bay for half the match. In the second half, the gates opened with Scholes scoring two and Ruud notching another to give United three more points for their title pursuit.

> **Man Utd 0–0 Man City**
> 07-11-2004
> **Newcastle Utd 1–3 Man Utd**
> 14-11-2004 (Rooney 2,
> van Nistelrooy pen.)
> **Man Utd 2–0 Charlton**
> 20-11-2004 (Giggs, Scholes)
> **West Bromwich 0–3 Man Utd**
> 27-11-2004 (Scholes 2,
> van Nistelrooy)

December 2004

Fresh from winning at West Brom in November, United faced some more struggling teams at Old Trafford in December. Sadly for their visitors, the Reds were not in the mood to give away priceless points – even if Christmas was just around the corner!

Southampton and Crystal Palace both made their long journeys home with nothing to show for their efforts. The Saints were sent packing in the second-half by goals from Paul Scholes, Wayne Rooney and Cristiano Ronaldo, who volleyed in the third with three minutes to go.

Palace were much pluckier when they visited Manchester a fortnight later.

Their goalkeeper Kiraly saved Rooney's penalty when the score was still 0–0, and even when they went 1–0 down to Scholes' goal, they soon equalised with Granville's stunning shot. Fortunately, the Reds were back in front, 2–1, before Fergie could give his team a half-time talking-to! Smith scored with a powerful header from Scholes' accurate corner.

The next three goals were scored in the first three minutes after half-time! Kolkka brought Palace level again, but then his team-mate Boyce put the ball in his own net. It had been 3–2 to United for only a minute when Scholes blasted in his second. Phew – what a start to the second-half! Old Trafford's digital scoreboard settled down at 4–2, until John O'Shea burst into the Palace box in the last minute and fired in United's fifth goal. It was a fitting end to a fantastic game.

Above: **Paul Scholes (centre) runs to congratulate Ryan Giggs for grabbing the goal in United's last game of 2004, away to Aston Villa.** Left: **Smith leaps like a salmon to score against Crystal Palace!**

Palace were perhaps unlucky to be in the wrong place – Old Trafford – at the wrong time – five days after United had been held to a frustrating draw at Fulham. There the Reds were set to win with Smith's goal, until Diop struck an unstoppable shot past Roy Carroll in the 88th minute. Ouch!

Happily, there were no such surprises in the two games closest to Christmas. Bolton were beaten 2–0 on Boxing Day with strikes by Scholes and Giggs. Ryan was flyin' – two days later, he played brilliantly at Villa Park, one of his favourite grounds, and scored the winning goal, United's last of 2004.

Man Utd 3–0 Southampton
04-12-2004 (Ronaldo, Scholes, Rooney)
Fulham 1–1 Man Utd
13-12-2004 (Smith)
Man Utd 5–2 Crystal Palace
18-12-2004 (Scholes 2, Smith, O'Shea, o.g.)
Man Utd 2–0 Bolton Wanderers
26-12-2004 (Giggs, Scholes)
Aston Villa 0–1 Man Utd
28-12-2004 (Giggs)

January 2005

Giggsy's great run didn't end with the old year, it continued in the new. He netted again at Middlesbrough on New Year's Day – although he was pipped to the pleasure of scoring United's first goal of 2005. Darren Fletcher did that, with his first goal for the club, in the 9th minute. It was a great moment for the young Scot and the perfect gift for his Scottish manager, Sir Alex Ferguson, who celebrated his birthday the day before on New Year's Eve.

Midfielders made the headlines at Middlesbrough but next it was the turn of the match officials. Fortunately their decision – or lack of one – favoured United, as it saved them from losing 0–1 at home to Spurs. That's what the final score should have been: TV cameras proved what most Reds fans had feared, that Mendes' long-range shot crossed the line before Roy Carroll clawed the ball out of his net. But the linesman failed to flag for a goal, the game carried on and it eventually finished 0–0!

If Carroll's blushes were spared, there was no such luck for Jerzy Dudek. For the third season in a row, the Liverpool goalkeeper dropped a clanger against United in front of his home crowd. Wayne Rooney was ever so grateful as his shot

Above: **"Watch and learn, son!" United captain Roy Keane gives Liverpool skipper Steven Gerrard a midfield masterclass.**

Below: **Louis Saha receives a warm welcome from Wayne Rooney after scoring against Villa.**

slipped through Dudek's hands – it gave the Reds a lead they defended admirably, especially after Wes Brown was sent off.

The same tactic which took care of Crystal Palace in December proved useful again in January, against Aston Villa. Two goals in the space of a minute, from Louis Saha and then Paul Scholes, won the game for United after they were pegged back by Barry's equaliser. Red-hot Ronaldo had opened the scoring much earlier, in the 8th minute. Fergie said: "Cristiano had his best game of the season for us. He was absolutely outstanding."

Middlesbrough 0–2 Man Utd
01-01-2005 (Fletcher, Giggs)
Man Utd 0–0 Tottenham Hotspur
04-01-2005
Liverpool 0–1 Man Utd
15-01-2005 (Rooney)
Man Utd 3–1 Aston Villa
22-01-2005 (Ronaldo, Saha, Scholes)

United Trivia

Paul Scholes made his 250th start in the Premiership on 22 January 2005, against Aston Villa. He celebrated the milestone by scoring his 124th goal for United in all competitions. Only three of Paul's team-mates have also netted more than 100 for the Reds: Ruud van Nistlerooy, Ryan Giggs and Ole Gunnar Solskjaer.

February 2005

If Fergie thought Ronaldo had his best game of the season against Aston Villa, he might have changed his mind 10 days later! On a storming night in North London, the Portuguese winger destroyed Arsenal with two goals in quick succession, early in the second-half. For more details on this amazing match, please turn to our **Best of Enemies** feature on pages 52–53.

Beating the Gunners away was a great achievement, but United fans knew the next game would be equally important. Some feared a Highbury hangover, having seen the Reds lose an easy game on paper (against Portsmouth) after their previous Premiership win over Arsenal.

Above: **Keane breaks the deadlock against Birmingham with his 50th goal for United. It was a busy period for Roy – see United Trivia opposite.**

This time, however, there'd be no such mistake. The youngest and oldest players on Fergie's team-sheet scored the goals in the 2–0 home win over Birmingham City. Roy Keane, aged 33, made the breakthrough 11 minutes after half-time with a strong run and powerful finish. Wayne Rooney, aged 19, doubled the score 11 minutes from the end with a skilful lob.

Rooney was the scourge of teams wearing blue shirts in February; he followed his goal against Birmingham with one in the Manchester derby and two at home to Portsmouth, as the Reds avenged their October defeat.

Wayne also set up United's other goal in their first win at City's new ground… scored by his former Everton team-mate Richard Dunne! The City centre-back tried to clear Rooney's cross but instead knocked the ball past his own goalkeeper, David James. Whoops!

United were made to wait for their next win, against Portsmouth. It all started so well, with the Reds going 1–0 up after only seven minutes. Ruud van Nistelrooy, back in the team after injury, made a nuisance of himself as Gary Neville's cross came over – and Rooney did the rest.

If the Old Trafford faithful expected it to be plain sailing after that, they were wrong. Pompey drew level with a long-range shot by O'Neil, two minutes after the

The 3 R's teach Portsmouth a lesson (L to R): **Ronaldo, Ryan and Rooney.**

interval, and then kept United at bay for half an hour. It was an anxious time for the home fans but finally, in the 81st minute, Rooney ran on to Ruud's pass and slotted in his second goal. Once again, Wayne was the match-winner – and the toast of a relieved Old Trafford.

Arsenal 2–4 Man Utd
01-02-2005 (Giggs, Ronaldo 2, O'Shea)
Man Utd 2–0 Birmingham City
05-02-2005 (Keane, Rooney)
Man City 0–2 Man Utd
13-02-2005 (Rooney, Dunne og)
Man Utd 2–1 Portsmouth
26-02-2005 (Rooney 2)

March 2005

A difficult trip to Milan in the UEFA Champions League, an FA Cup tie at Southampton and a ten-day break for World Cup qualifiers meant March was a quiet month for Manchester United in the Premiership… just when the season would normally be hotting up!

The distractions didn't help United in their quest to catch Chelsea in the title race. Sir Alex Ferguson's side, so prolific in the previous month, scored only one goal in two league games against teams in the bottom half of the table.

Cristiano Ronaldo's curling shot in the 21st minute was enough to beat Fulham at home but only just. The visitors had some good chances to score in the second-half; Tim Howard had to be sharp to stop players like Cole, the former Old Trafford favourite, from repeating history and scoring an equaliser. Fulham had held United to an unlikely draw in December and they came mighty close to doing it again in mid-March.

The previous Premiership performance, away to Crystal Palace, was even more disappointing. If the Reds had won, they would have been just three points behind the league leaders; instead, their 0–0 draw, followed by Chelsea's win at Norwich, widened the gap again to eight points.

The failure to score at Selhurst Park was baffling, especially after Fergie had brought on Ronaldo, Wayne Rooney and Paul Scholes as substitutes in the second-half. The Reds even had an extra-man advantage for the last 25 minutes, after Lakis was sent off for a foul on Keane.

It clearly wasn't meant to be United's day. And it didn't look as if it would be their season either, not to the frustrated fans who made the long journey home from London to Manchester. They knew the Reds would need an amazing April to turn the title race around.

United Trivia

Roy Keane reached two milestones in his Manchester United career during February and March. First, he scored his 50th goal for the club in the 2–0 win at home to Birmingham City. The skipper then made his 300th Premiership start for the Reds in the goalless draw at Crystal Palace.

Crystal Palace 0–0 Man Utd
05-03-2005
Man Utd 1–0 Fulham
19-03-2005 (Ronaldo)

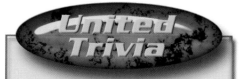

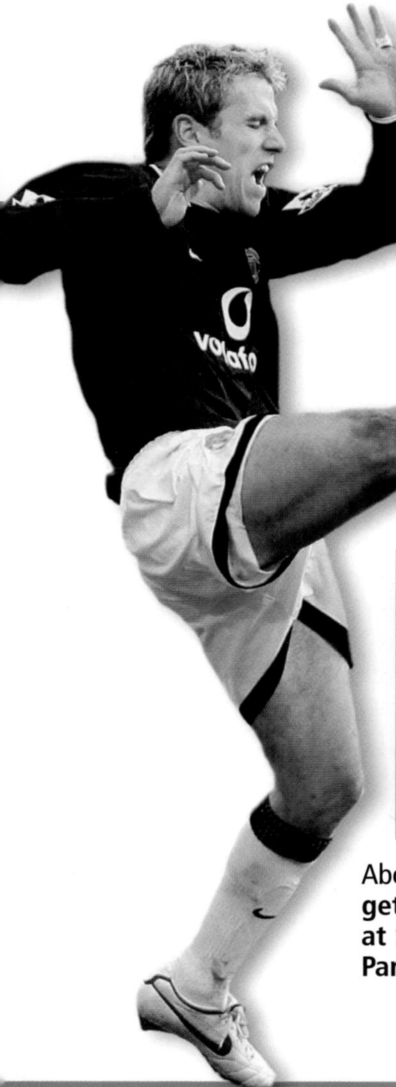

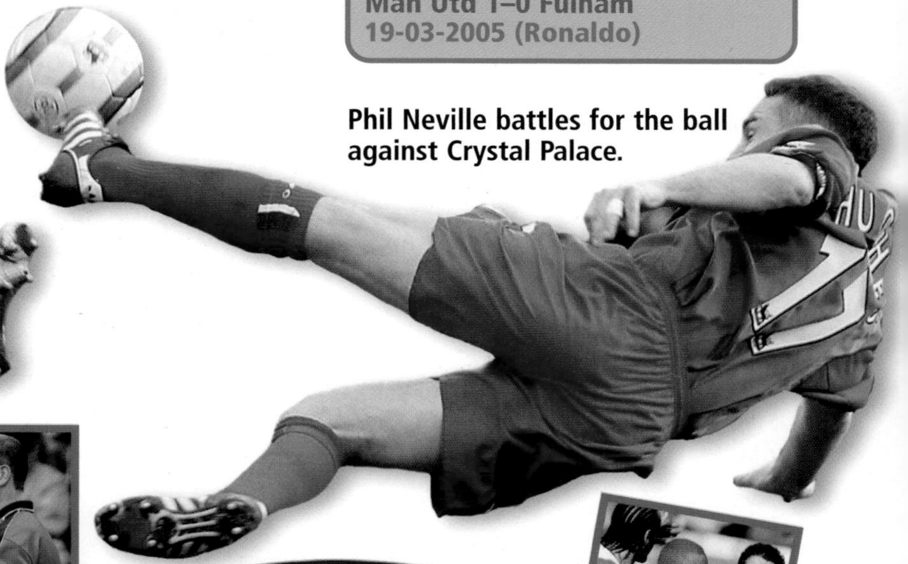

Phil Neville battles for the ball against Crystal Palace.

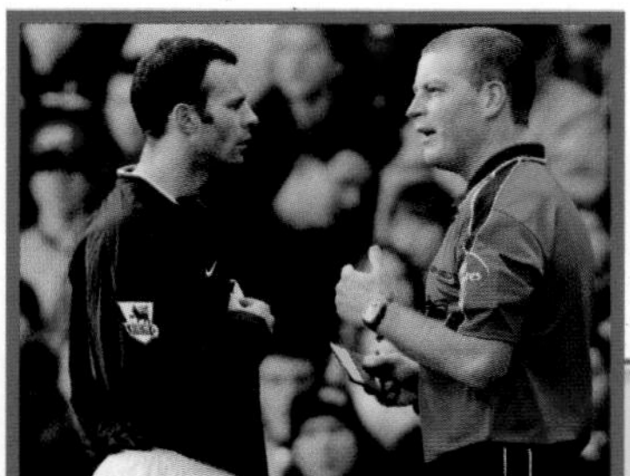

Above: **Giggs gets booked at Selhurst Park.**

United Trivia

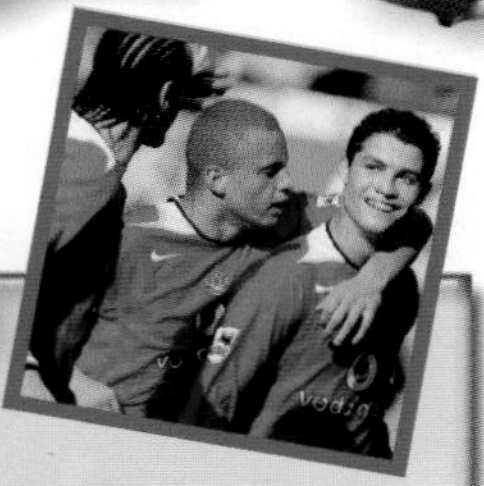

Wes Brown (picture right with Ronaldo) made his 100th Premiership start against Crystal Palace. The versatile defender clocked up most of those appearances at centre-back, alongside the likes of Rio Ferdinand and Mikael Silvestre. But at Selhurst Park, Wes coverered for the injured Gary Neville at right-back.

April 2005

In some respects, April was an amazing month. It was amazing, for example, that United scored six goals in two games against Newcastle – but didn't score any in the battles with Blackburn, Norwich and Everton!

Blackburn Rovers were the first team to frustrate the Reds, holding them to their ninth 0–0 draw of the season. Brad Friedel was in fine form at Old Trafford, just as he'd been at Ewood Park in August. He made two brilliant saves to stop Mikael Silvestre and Wayne Rooney from scoring; Silvestre also had a header cleared off the line by a defender, while Rooney (crossbar) and Ronaldo (post) both hit the woodwork. Unlucky!

If there was one thing the Reds didn't need in April, it was a repeat of their March performance at Crystal Palace. Sadly, there were similarities with the trip to Norwich but this time, the outcome was much worse! Again, three of Fergie's best attacking players started on the bench; again, they failed to turn the game around when they came on. Ronaldo was first into the fray after 22 minutes, followed by Rooney at half-time. And when Ruud van

Gary Neville enjoyed many great moments during his first three hundred league games for United. But the milestone match itself – number 300 – is one he'd rather forget! On a difficult night against Everton, Gary was sent off for losing his cool and kicking the ball into the crowd at Goodison Park.

Nistelrooy replaced Kleberson, he was only on the field for three minutes before Norwich scored their decisive second goal. Ashton (55') and McKenzie (66') left United stuck on 67 points.

The next match could hardly have been more different – see page 25 for details of United's win over Newcastle in the FA Cup semi-final. But the game after that, away to Rooney's old club Everton, was more in line with United's lean spell. The dismal 1–0 defeat was compounded by two red cards for Gary Neville (see United Trivia above) and Paul Scholes (fouls on Arteta, Kilbane).

At least April ended on a high, with another game against Newcastle. The Magpies' hopes of revenge were raised when Ambrose gave them the lead but ruined when Rooney's wonder-volley rocketed past Given in the Newcastle goal. The visitors might have settled for a score draw but even that was snatched from them when Wes Brown headed home the winner.

Cleared for take-off! Wes Brown uses his aerial ability to good effect in scoring United's winning goal against Newcastle.

Man Utd 0–0 Blackburn
02-04-2005
Norwich 2–0 Man Utd
09-04-2005
Everton 1–0 Man Utd
20-04-2005
Man Utd 2–1 Newcastle
24-04-2005 (Rooney, Brown)

Ryan Giggs celebrates his goal with John O'Shea and Phil Neville, despite the protests from West Brom's Zoltan Gera (far right)!

May 2005

United could have picked a better time to produce their biggest league win of the 2004/05 season. Beating your opponents by four goals at their ground is impressive, but coming just 24 hours after Chelsea had clinched the Premiership title at Bolton, it seemed like a case of 'too little, too late'.

However, second place was still up for grabs and with that target in mind, Fergie's men in black blasted Charlton 4–0 at The Valley. Paul Scholes and Darren Fletcher registered their first league goals since January as United took control before half-time. Alan Smith then took his season's tally into double figures before Wayne Rooney rounded things off.

Only the woodwork and some good saves by Charlton's new Danish goalkeeper Andersen prevented Rooney from scoring his first hat-trick in the Premiership… let's hope Wayne won't have to wait much longer for it!

In their next match United faced a striker who did score a hat-trick away to Charlton: West Bromwich Albion's Robert Earnshaw. But even though the Welsh international bagged three goals in 17 minutes at The Valley, few people expected him or his team-mates to get even one at Old Trafford.

The Reds were rampant in the first half, with Ryan Giggs and Cristiano Ronaldo causing plenty of problems for the team propping up the Premiership

table. West Brom looked to be in real trouble when their number one shot-stopper Hoult limped off the field, shortly after Giggs curled a free-kick past him in the 21st minute. But far from being overawed, the visitors' substitute goalie Kuszczak played a blinder, keeping the score at 1–0 until his side managed to grab a shock penalty equaliser.

Earnshaw scored it, after the ref spotted an apparent foul in the box by O'Shea on Horsfield. Fergie responded by making a triple substitution: Rooney, Saha and Scholes replaced Kleberson, Phil Neville and Smith. The changes nearly paid off – Scholes hit a fierce

Darren Fletcher celebrated in style when he clocked up his 50th start for United's first team – by scoring in the 4–0 win at Charlton. By the end of the season, Fletch had three goals to his name – and the talented young Scot bagged all three away from home and all when the Reds were wearing the black kit!

shot in the 86th minute, only to see it hit the post. The frustrating 1–1 draw all but handed the runners-up spot to Arsenal. Fergie was furious!

From one end of the table to another… just three days later, Old Trafford welcomed the top team in England. Sir Alex ordered his men to applaud as Chelsea walked onto the field. Later, the same players saluted their supporters, as United performed their traditional lap of honour in their final home match. In between, there was little for the Reds fans to cheer about, apart from Ruud van Nistelrooy's opening goal in the 7th minute. Otherwise, the night belonged to the new champions, who won 3–1 thanks to Gudjohnsen, Tiago and Joe Cole.

With the top four places all decided, the TV cameras turned to the bottom of the table on the last day of the Premiership season. United played their part on an enthralling afternoon; goals by Fletcher and Van Nistelrooy relegated Southampton, while West Brom beat Portsmouth to survive. Norwich and Crystal Palace also went down with the Saints… thus saving the Reds from making three of their longest league journeys in 2005/06!

Charlton 0–4 Man Utd
01-05-2005 (Scholes, Fletcher, Smith, Rooney)
Man Utd 1–1 West Brom
07-05-2005 (Giggs)
Man Utd 1–3 Chelsea
10-05-2005 (van Nistelrooy)
Southampton 1–2 Man Utd
15-05-2005 (Fletcher, van Nistelrooy)

The TOTAL FOOTBALLER
Rooney

Wayne Rooney

Date of birth: 24 October 1985
Birthplace: Liverpool
**Date signed: 31 August 2004,
from Everton**
**United debut: v Fenerbahce
(Champions League),
28 September 2004**

Wayne Rooney made one of the most remarkable debuts of all time when he first wore the red shirt of Manchester United. It came almost a month after he signed for the club, but it was well worth the wait – Wayne scored a hat-trick in the 6–2 thrashing of Fenerbahce in UEFA Champions League Group D. It was an electric start to his Old Trafford career; all three goals were in the bag by the 54th minute!

After such a breathtaking beginning, many people wondered what Wayne would do next. How on earth do you follow a hat-trick in your first game? Not easily was the answer, as Middlesbrough, Birmingham and Sparta Prague all proved, stopping him from scoring in his second, third and fourth matches. But the kid from Croxteth, Liverpool, wouldn't be kept out of the headlines for too long. In game number five, he gained even more street-cred in Stretford, Manchester by sinking United's arch-rivals Arsenal. Not only did he score, he also won the penalty which Ruud van Nistelrooy gladly converted. Even better, the Reds' 2–0 win ended Arsenal's 49-match unbeaten run. And if any icing on the cake was needed, it was also Wayne's 19th birthday!

The teenager gave Manchester United fans three more goals to enjoy

before Christmas, including two in one of United's most impressive away wins of the season – 3–1 against Newcastle.

Sometimes the toughest matches bring out the best in players, and they don't come much tougher than away matches against Newcastle, Liverpool and Manchester City! Rooney scored in all three of those fixtures in his first season at Manchester United.

Wayne's winning goal at Anfield in January was especially sweet; the Liverpool fans had given him all sorts of stick for switching from Everton to their other major enemy. Slotting the ball past their goalkeeper was the perfect way to respond. The same month saw Wayne score three more goals, all in the FA Cup – one against Exeter City in the third round replay and two at home to Middlesbrough in round four.

Rooney received his first award as a United player in February 2005 when he was named Barclays Player of the Month. He scored four goals in the Premiership against Portsmouth (2), Manchester City and Birmingham.

Fergie, who was named Manager of the Month, said at the time: "Wayne's form has been absolutely fantastic and he thoroughly deserves the award. The Portsmouth game emphasised the form he's in. It also highlighted the improvement he's making as a player. Every week he seems to be adding something to his game."

Wayne added another personal honour to his CV in April 2005. His fellow professionals voted him the PFA Young Player of the Year, an award previously won by Ryan Giggs in 1992 and 1993, and David Beckham in 1997.

Quotes on Wayne Rooney ...

"Rooney can shoot from distance, get on the end of crosses, hit free-kicks – anything. He has the sort of forward's instinct which you cannot buy and no coach can teach. You are born with it. I would pay to watch him play."
THIERRY HENRY, ARSENAL FORWARD

"Would I like to work with Wayne Rooney? Who wouldn't want to work with him? We all like to work with exceptional talent."
ARSENE WENGER, ARSENAL MANAGER

"He is a total footballer. He can play anywhere, in midfield, up front, but perhaps we won't put him in the back four just yet! Probably his best position is just behind the striker. He has the ability to beat men which is important if you're playing there."
SIR ALEX FERGUSON

... on Wayne's United Debut

"To score a hat-trick on your full debut is what dreams are made of. Not only that, his overall performance was outstanding. I think you will find it very hard to find a better debut than that. The way he carried himself was just brilliant."
RYAN GIGGS

"If I could pick out one thing that sets him apart, it would be his attitude. He knew all eyes were going to be on him but he just went out there and did his own thing. That shows incredible character, especially at his age. In that sense, he's fearless."
RUUD VAN NISTELROOY

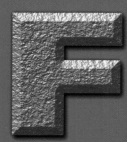

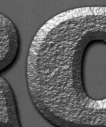
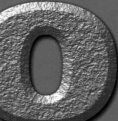

Smith

The FRONT

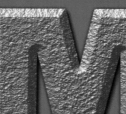

Saha MEN

VanNistelrooy

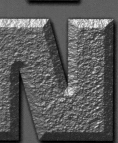

Ruud van Nistelrooy

Date of birth: 1 July 1976
Birthplace: Oss, Holland
Date signed: 1 July 2001, from PSV Eindhoven
United debut: v Liverpool (Community Shield), 12 Aug '01

"Van Nistelrooy is the best, most clinical finisher we've ever had here." So says United manager Sir Alex Ferguson, and there can be no better introduction to the club's prolific Dutch marksman. Ruud surpassed Denis Law's haul of 28 goals in Europe – a record that had stood for 36 years – when he scored the first of two goals against Lyon in September 2004, in the Champions League.

Law, dubbed 'The King' during his Old Trafford playing days in the 60s and 70s was clinical to say the least. The Scottish forward scored 236 goals in 393 United appearances. Law scored 28 goals in 33 European appearances, but van Nistelrooy notched his 29th and 30th slightly quicker, in 32 games. And the deadly Dutchman shows no signs of slowing down his phenomenal goal-scoring rate.

Ruud joined the club in 2001 having overcome a serious knee injury sustained at his previous club PSV. He had been set to sign for United a year previously, but the injury postponed his arrival at Old Trafford. Ferguson's reassuring words in that difficult time proved influential; when the Dutchman had recovered, he repaid Ferguson's loyalty by joining the Reds for £19 million, rejecting a late offer from Real Madrid.

The manager's persistence was justified as Ruud broke the 30-goal barrier in his first three seasons with the club. "His record is fantastic," Sir Alex fittingly concludes. "Ruud is the best in Europe. His record has been incredible from the moment he joined us."

Louis Saha

Date of birth: 8 August 1978
Birthplace: Paris
Date signed: 23 January 2004, from Fulham
United debut: v Southampton (Premiership), 31 Jan '04

Louis Saha began his football career with French side Metz, and got his first taste of English football with a four-month loan spell at Newcastle in 1999. Saha returned to Metz, but a year later came back to England when Fulham signed him for £2.1 million. The 6ft 1in striker played more than 100 Premiership matches for the Cottagers, scoring a total of 53 goals.

Saha was the first of three strikers to arrive at Old Trafford in 2004 when he signed from Fulham in January for £12.8m. The early part of the striker's United career was besieged by bad luck – in his second season, he had two spells on the sidelines after being injured while playing for France. When he's fit, Saha adds speed and power to the talented front quartet Sir Alex has at his disposal. And fans will recall he scored six goals in his first eight games for the Reds as he struck up a potent partnership with Ruud van Nistelrooy.

The Parisian striker possesses great pace and an aerial presence enhanced by his extraordinarily high leap. In Ruud, Rooney, Saha and Smith, United have one of the deadliest strike-forces in Europe. If Saha can end his poor luck with injuries he is capable of making a significant contribution to United's attack – and we all know what happened the last time Sir Alex had four top strikers to choose from...

Alan Smith

Date of birth: 28 October 1980
Birthplace: Wakefield, Yorkshire
Date signed: 27 May 2004, from Leeds United
United debut: v Arsenal (Community Shield), 8 Aug '04

When Alan Smith made the move across the Pennines that divide Manchester and Leeds, there was no small amount of controversy. There were the Leeds fans, of course, who were bitterly disappointed to see their heroic, hometown boy make the switch to their fiercest rivals. Then there were United fans, who pondered: "Would this Yorkshire-born-and-bred lad ever be as committed in a Red shirt?" and "Is he a clinical enough finisher?"; he'd scored nine goals in Leeds' relegation season of 2003/04 – admittedly from a midfield position.

Smith answered the latter question in his first six games for the Reds, scoring five goals. But it was his wholehearted devotion to United's cause that quickly earned him a place in the hearts of the fans. Smith's no-nonsense, all-action, fully-committed style is displayed perfectly in the goal he scored against Fulham in December 2004. Against most other forwards, Fulham's Sylvain Legwinski would have had ample time to select the correct pass out of defence. Not against Smith. The determined forward steamed in with a full-blooded challenge, reclaimed the ball and coolly slotted his finish past Edwin van der Saar.

Such defiance and determination has made fans worship Roy Keane, and Bryan Robson before him. Any initial doubts about Smith were hurriedly forgotten and never mentioned again.

United's
QUIET
MAN
Scholes

Paul Scholes is Manchester United's quiet man, a rare breed of footballer who prefers the Premiership without the premières, the football without the photoshoots.

There are few players in the game who command respect and admiration so readily. But praise isn't something Scholes craves. "Compliments are nice," he once said in an interview, "but I'd rather not get them. I'd rather people talked about someone else. I've done all right and I've managed to score a few goals with United, but I'd never say to myself 'I'm a good player'."

Any young player hoping to learn from football's masters could do worse than monitor Scholes during a game. Always aware of the whereabouts of team-mates and opposition, he has his next pass mapped out in his head before he has even received the ball. His passing is exemplary, his finishing sublime. Scholes can time his run into the opposition penalty area with exact precision, whilst his technique for striking the ball is like clockwork in motion.

But he is never one to sing his own praises. So, in celebration of eleven seasons as the Reds' silent assassin, we'll let others do the talking for him, including Sir Alex and some ex-United heroes…

"There is not a player in the land as good as he is. He has control, composure, vision, awareness. He is absolutely magnificent and for me one of the greatest players in the game."

"Not being interested in the limelight is what makes Paul such a special person."

"Scholes is a genius. He ghosts into goal-scoring positions and is so difficult to pick up."
SIR ALEX FERGUSON

"Paul Scholes impressed me most when I first arrived at United. Watching his all-round play in training, he's unbelievable; he's someone you'd always want in your team."
WAYNE ROONEY

"One of the players that I most like playing against, somebody who I think is more intelligent than most other players, is Paul Scholes. He has an intelligence, a reading of the game that is way above most other players."
PATRICK VIEIRA, ARSENAL MIDFIELDER

"Paul Scholes is truly exceptional; the one player who can do everything – defend and attack, pass the ball and dribble past people. His most priceless asset is that he is always where he should be at the right time. In my opinion, he is the best English player."
LAURENT BLANC, FORMER TEAM-MATE

"I played with Paul from the age of 15 and he is one of the country's best-ever players. I respect him as a person and as a footballer."
DAVID BECKHAM, FORMER TEAM-MATE

"He makes it look so easy, doesn't he? There is not a better midfield player in the world. He is not only a midfield player, he is a midfield goal-scorer. How Scholes hasn't been named in the top six for European Player of the Year is an absolute disgrace. Thierry Henry was disappointed he didn't get top spot but Scholes is equally as good as him."

"He keeps himself to himself and doesn't promote himself as the superstar that he is. That's probably why he has been overlooked. When he receives a pass he isn't ball-watching. He's looking where he is going to be passing it and that's one of the reasons why he is so good."
SAM ALLARDYCE, BOLTON WANDERERS MANAGER

"Scholes is one of the most naturally gifted English players of all time."
GEORGE BEST

"He's a true football player and things happen around him. He makes the midfield tick and does everything – delicate little touches, long passes, short passes, switching the play. He's a football player, that's it."
SVEN GORAN ERIKSSON, ENGLAND MANAGER

Paul Scholes
Date of birth: **16 Nov 1974**
Born: **Salford**
Height: **170 cm**
Signed trainee forms at United: **8 July 1991**
Signed professional: **23 January 1993**
United debut: **v Port Vale, (League Cup) 21 September 1994**

"He has a very special talent. It was a privilege just to work so closely with him."
SVEN GORAN ERIKSSON, ENGLAND MANAGER

"He simply has the best football brain I'd ever seen in a young kid. Let's face it, Scholes is in a class of his own."
BRIAN KIDD, FORMER UNITED ASSISTANT MANAGER

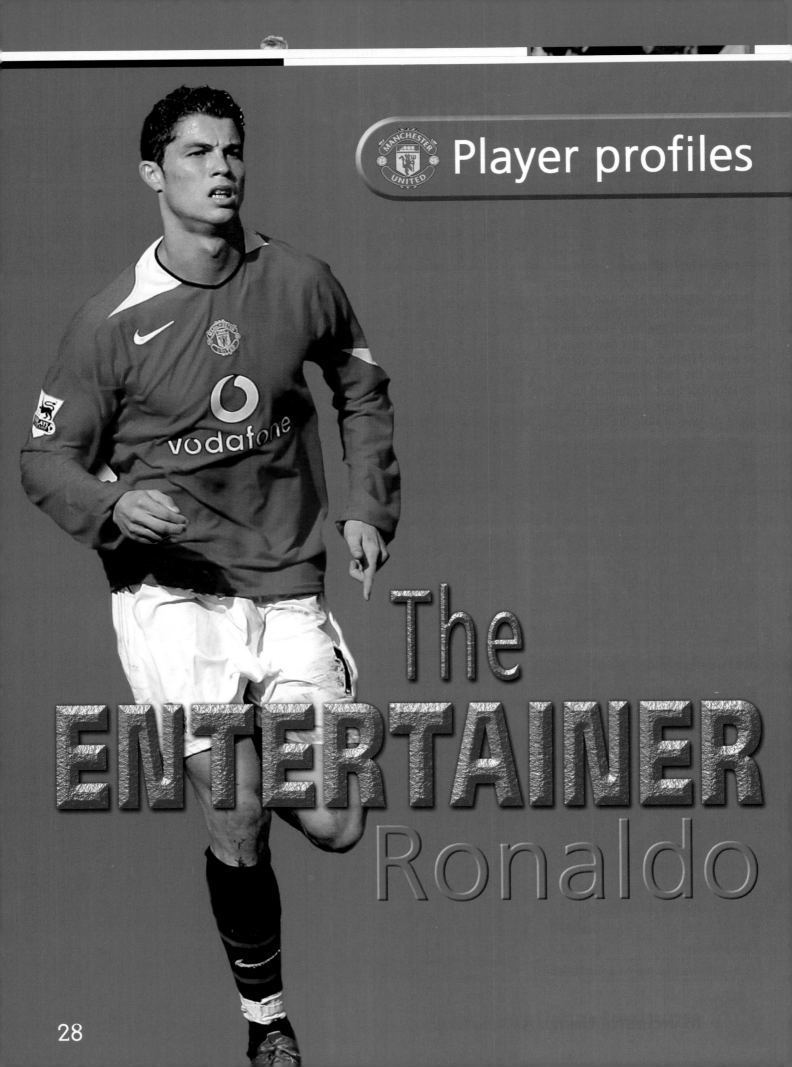

The ENTERTAINER Ronaldo

28

Cristiano Ronaldo

Date of birth: 5 February 1985
Birthplace: Madeira, Portugal
Date signed: 12 August 2003,
from Sporting Lisbon
United debut: v Bolton
(Premiership), 11 September 2003

It's 12 August 2003, and the reception area of Manchester United's training ground is full of journalists waiting to put their questions to Sir Alex Ferguson ahead of a Champions League qualifying match with Zalaegerzegi.

The press are aware that United have signed the talented but relatively unknown Portuguese winger Cristiano Ronaldo from Sporting Lisbon. But an official announcement and confirmation of the fee isn't due until that afternoon. Brazilian superstar Ronaldinho has been United's main transfer target during the summer, so Christiano's arrival has largely slipped under the radar of the TV, press and radio reporters.

When copies of the official statement containing details of the transfer are handed out to all the waiting journalists, there is no shortage of shock. A look at the size of the fee – £12.24m – leaves one surprised reporter asking, "How good exactly is this kid?"

The surprise didn't end there. In the statement, Sir Alex Ferguson said this: "He is one of the most exciting young players I have ever seen." Such praise isn't handed out lightly by the United boss.

Ronaldo's self-confidence was evident right from the start. Asked whether he thought of himself as a player for the future, he said: "No, from now I would like to make an immediate impact and make sure the people that have put faith in me are proved right." And they were.

United supporters desperate to see the club's new No.7 – the shirt David Beckham had recently vacated after joining Real Madrid - had to wait a month for Ronaldo's debut. His first appearance for the Reds finally arrived against Bolton, on 11 September. 67,000 jack-in-a-box fans were off their seats in anticipation every time Ronaldo touched the ball. A 61st minute substitute, Ronaldo gave a brief but brilliant taste of what was to come.

Twelve months later, he received a nice addition to his FA Cup winners' medal – the Sir Matt Busby Player of the Year award, as voted for by United members.

Ronaldo learned many of his incredible skills and tricks – including step-overs, quick turns and dribbling at speed – on the streets of Madeira, the Portuguese island where he grew up before moving to the big city of Lisbon.

"My tricks are all down to playing football on the streets," he explains. "I used to play football in every spare second of the day. Me and my friends used to eat, drink and breathe football." His confidence to beat players was obvious even then. "I always felt the belief that if you put one man or five

Ronaldo torments Everton during an FA Cup tie in February 2005.

men in front of me, I could go past them all," he adds.

Ronaldo continues to improve his all-round game. Some of his performances in 2004/05 showed how much he is maturing on the field – he now uses his tricks at the right times. And his shots and crosses are deadlier than ever!

The accolades from his manager keep coming, too. United may have missed out on Ronaldinho in 2003, but Sir Alex is convinced that during that summer he signed a player who, alongside Wayne Rooney, can be every bit as good as the talented Brazilian in years to come.

"I think Cristiano and Wayne will be the best in the world alongside Ronaldinho at Barcelona. They will both be world-class."

United fans have plenty to look forward to from this exciting showman.

Quotes on Ronaldo ...

"He's got a fantastic personality, a great strength of mind and a sense of purpose. Those things will help him more than anything and take him really far in the game."
SIR ALEX FERGUSON

"There are players who raise their game to a new level. They see things that I, as their manager, cannot see. Ronaldo will be one of those players, just like Cantona before him."
SIR ALEX FERGUSON

"Ronaldo is a fantastic player. He is improving all the time. His end product is there and he's scoring goals now too."
RUUD VAN NISTELROOY

"Cristiano Ronaldo has magic in his boots and I'm delighted he has signed for Manchester United. That is where Ronaldo should be if he wants to become a truly great player."
EUSEBIO, PORTUGAL LEGEND

"There are things he does with the ball that make me scratch my head and wonder how he did it. It must be terrifying to be a defender against him."
LUIS FIGO, PORTUGAL LEGEND

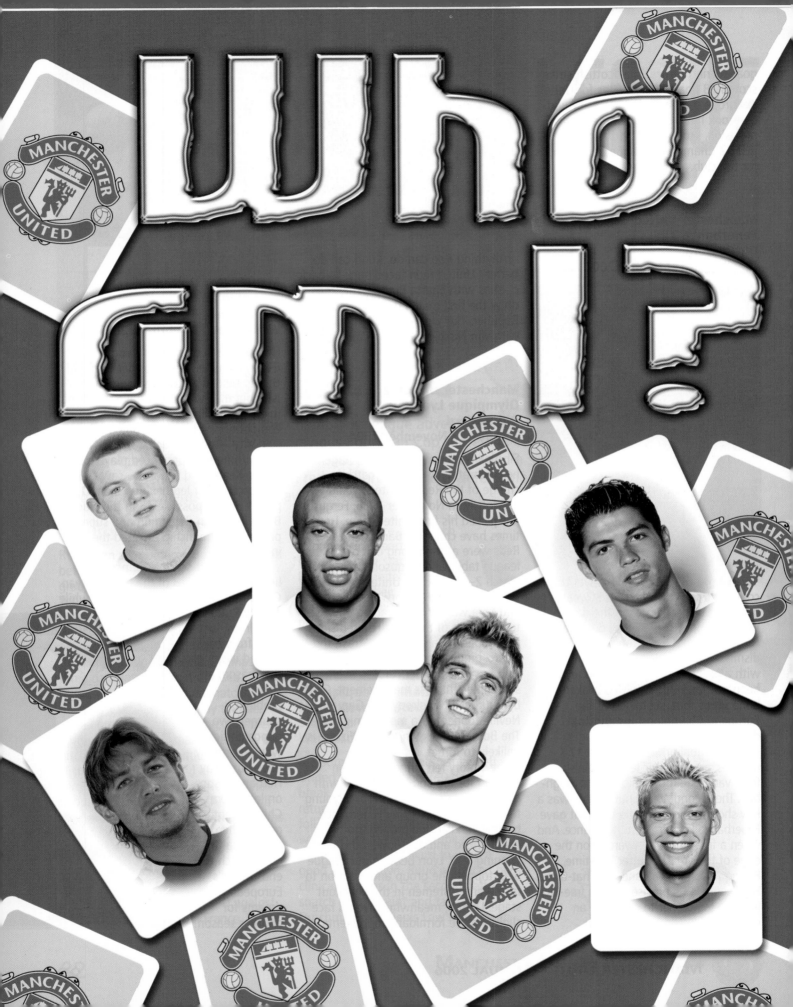

The faces of Manchester United's players are instantly recognisable to the club's fans all around the world. But do you know your favourite footballers well enough to identify them from our five clues?

Who Am I?

- I am an Olympic gold medallist
- I joined United from Paris Saint Germain for £6.9m in June 2004
- I have only played 8 times in my home nation's domestic league
- My middle name is Ivan
- I scored my first goal for United, against Bolton in September 2004

Answer:

Who Am I?

- I was born in Chambray-les-Tours
- I began my career with Rennes
- I joined United in September 1999
- I played in Serie A with Inter Milan
- My first red card for United came in our 4–2 win over Arsenal in 2005

Answer:

Who Am I?

- I joined the club at the age of 16
- I was born in Mayfield
- I made my United debut against FC Basel in March 2003
- I was made captain of my country at the age of 20
- I scored my first United goal against Middlesbrough in January 2005

Answer:

Who Am I?

- I scored on my United debut against Arsenal in the 2004 Community Shield
- I play in an attacking position, but I enjoy a crunching 50/50 tackle
- I used to play at Elland Road
- I made my England debut against Mexico in 2001
- I wear the number 14 shirt

Answer:

Who Am I?

- I made my United debut against Bolton in August 2003
- I wear the shirt number previously worn by Cantona and Beckham
- I signed for United shortly after playing against them in a friendly
- I earned 17 caps and scored 7 goals for my country before I turned 20
- I was born on the island of Madeira

Answer:

Who Am I?

- I used to wear blue in home games
- Paul Gascoigne and Alan Shearer are my football idols
- I am my nation's youngest-ever debutant (aged 17 years 111 days)
- I scored four goals in four games at Euro 2004
- I made my debut for United against a team from Istanbul

Answer:

Can you do an OLE?

Ole Gunnar Solskjaer celebrates his tenth year with Manchester United in 2006. The term 'super-sub' really doesn't do Ole justice. However, one of the Norwegian's undoubted talents is his ability to study the game from the dug-out and decide what's needed to turn a game. We've picked five past games where Sir Alex Ferguson's men required a comeback. All you have to do is use your United knowledge and tell us who scored the last goal in each of the games. Give yourself a point for each one you get right. Answers are on page 60.

Manchester United 2
Bayern Munich 1
26 May 1999, European Cup Final
Nou Camp, Barcelona

After just six minutes, Mario Basler gives Bayern Munich the lead and the Germans protect their advantage to go in 1–0 up at half-time. United twice survive Bayern hitting the woodwork, but time is running out for the Reds. Then, just as the game enters injury time, substitute Teddy Sheringham levels the scores with a dramatic equaliser. But the comeback doesn't end there. David Beckham swings in a corner, Teddy flicks it on, but who gets the crucial touch?

Who scored the winner in Barcelona?

Tottenham 3
Manchester United 5
29 September 2001,
Premiership, White Hart Lane

Dean Richards, Les Ferdinand and Christian Ziege give Tottenham an unlikely 3–0 half-time lead. Teddy Sheringham, playing for Spurs at the time, warns his ecstatic team-mates to expect the United cavalry to arrive. It certainly does. Andy Cole, Laurent Blanc and Ruud van Nistelrooy respond in 27 exhilarating second-half minutes to make it 3–3. Juan Sebastian Veron put the Reds in front for the first time, but which London lad secures a memorable 5–3 victory at the Lane?

Who scored United's fifth?

Above: **Ruud prepares to come on as sub in a European match.**

West Ham 3
Manchester United 5
16 March 2002,
Premiership, Upton Park

A see-saw first half sees Steve Lomas put West Ham 1–0 up, David Beckham equalise for United, Freddie Kanoute put West Ham 2–1 and Nicky Butt equalise. In the second half Solskjaer crosses for Scholes to make it 3–2 before the Norwegian forward gets on the scoresheet himself. The 4–2 lead doesn't last long as Jermain Defoe pegs one back for the home side. However, all three points in an epic Premiership encounter are secured from the penalty spot, but which Reds midfielder puts the spot-kick away?

Who scored United's fifth?

Solskjaer Statistics

Date of birth: **26 February 1973**
Birthplace: **Kristiansund, Norway**
Date signed: **29 July 1996, from Molde (Norway)**
United debut: **v Blackburn (Premiership), 25 August 1996**

A knee ligament injury kept Ole out for the entire season in 2004/05, leaving him stuck on 199 starts for United. Rarely did a game pass during the season without Reds fans singing the striker's name, while a '20 Legend' flag remains draped over the first tier of the Stretford End at Old Trafford.

Juventus 2
Manchester United 3
21 April 1999,
Champions League
Semi-final 2nd leg
Stadio delle Alpi

Filippo Inzaghi scores twice in the opening ten minutes to put Juve 2–0 up. Keane begins the revival after 24 minutes with a glancing header, before Dwight Yorke equalises to make it 2–2 at half-time. The Reds are winning the tie on away goals after drawing 1–1 at Old Trafford. But there's time just to make absolutely certain in the 84th minute…

Who scored the winner in Turin?

Manchester United 2
Liverpool 1
24 January 1999,
FA Cup 4th Round, Old Trafford

Michael Owen puts Liverpool 1–0 up after just three minutes of this FA Cup tie. The Anfield Reds look as if they're going to hold out and progress to the fifth round as the clock shows just two minutes remaining. But, just in the nick of time, Dwight Yorke pokes the ball over the line to make it 1–1. The momentum is now with the home team.

But which United forward comes off the bench to settle this cup match with an injury-time winner?

What's Your Score?

0 points – The manager wants to use you as a substitute late in the game but you realise you've forgotten your boots. You are transfer-listed the next day!

1 point – Sir Alex calls on you for the last five minutes. Your first touch puts you one-on-one with the keeper, but you trip over your shoelaces! It's a chance missed.

2 points – Ferguson recognises it's time to bring you on with five minutes remaining. You create an opening and hit the post with a long-range shot. So close. Unlucky!

3 points – United are losing 1–0 and Fergie must rescue a vital point as the title race gathers pace. You come on and beat the keeper with a classy finish. 1–1. Job done.

4 points – It's the last game of the season, the title decider against Chelsea at Old Trafford and the game is all square at 2–2. Ferguson gives you the nod, you come on and score with a bicycle kick from the edge of the area. 3–2. Champions!

5 points – It's the European Cup final, United are going for an unprecedented Quadruple, but the Reds are 2–0 down to AC Milan and running out of time. You leave the bench, bag a hat-trick and return home a hero.

Left: **Can Wayne win the match for United? Sir Alex certainly hopes so!**

Ferdinand

BACKBONE BOYS

Howard

Tim Howard

Date of birth: 3 June 1979
Birthplace: New Jersey, USA
Date signed: 15 July 2003, from NY/NJ MetroStars
United debut: v Arsenal (Community Shield), 10 August 2003

Even the best players can have difficult second seasons with a football club, for several reasons. The adrenalin and excitement of making their debut has long since faded; opponents have started to suss them out; fans aren't as forgiving when they make mistakes. So it proved with Rio Ferdinand in 2003/04, and then with Tim Howard in 2004/05. But while Rio's spell on the sidelines was due to a momentary lapse of memory (remember? he forgot to attend a drugs test), Tim's absence from the team was caused by a temporary loss of form. Mistakes in the back-to-back matches away to Bolton and Lyon in September 2004 – both of which ended in 2–2 draws – saw the American lose his regular place to his good friend but rival Roy Carroll.

"I didn't do my job to the best of my ability," admitted Tim, later in the season. "You are always going to have dips and blips in form. It's about how you manage them and minimise them, and how you get back on the upswing."

For Tim, the only way to bounce back was to work hard on the training ground and to impress on the pitch when he was recalled for the Carling Cup and FA Cup matches. He didn't play in the Premiership for five months – but returned for the 2–1 win over Portsmouth in February, three days after Carroll's unfortunate error allowed Hernan Crespo to score for AC Milan in the first leg at Old Trafford.

Howard stayed in the side for the second leg, and was beaten by the same player – Crespo scored at the San Siro with a looping header. But that was the only goal that Tim conceded in a run of six games throughout March and into early April. He kept clean sheets away to Crystal Palace, Southampton and Norwich, and in the home matches against Fulham and Blackburn. His performance against Fulham was especially solid and included a brilliant second-half save to stop Carlos Bocanegra, his USA team-mate, from equalising for the visitors.

Some of the newspapers preferred to ignore Tim's impressive return, insisting the Reds would hunt high and low for new talent to replace him at the end of the season. Ever-determined, Tim told United's match programme: "I would love to play for this club for the rest of my career and cement myself in this club the way Keano, Scholesy, Ryan, Gary and Phil have. That's my goal."

Rio Ferdinand

Date of birth: 7 November 1978
Birthplace: Peckham, London
Date signed: 22 July 2002, from Leeds United
United debut: v Zalaegerszeg (Champions League qualifier), 27 August 2002

Rio Ferdinand received a hero's welcome when he returned to action in September 2004. Like Eric Cantona nine years before him, the defender made his comeback against United's old rivals Liverpool at Old Trafford. His manager and team-mates were delighted to see him on the field again after an eight-month suspension. "Rio was immense," said Sir Alex Ferguson, after the match. "It wasn't so much what he did as the influence he had on the rest of the side." The influence he had on his central defensive partner, Silvestre, was certainly positive – the Frenchman scored both of United's goals! No disrespect to the other defenders, but maybe Mikael felt more relaxed with Rio at his side. As if to say, "Right, now he's back, I can go and attack!"

Of course, Ferdinand himself isn't famous for attacking and scoring. At the time of writing this, he was still waiting for his first United goal – having netted only four goals in seven years with his previous clubs Leeds and West Ham. But few people can fault Rio's ability for preventing goals. His ball-reading skills and strong tackle make him a formidable obstacle for any forwards who fancy their chances against the Reds. Sometimes, a striker will get lucky and catch Rio or one of his colleagues on an off-day. But more often than not, his opponents go away empty-handed and shaking their heads at the task of getting past the kingpin of United's back four.

"We were banging our heads against a brick wall," said Gordon Strachan, when his Southampton team failed to score against United in February 2003. "Rio Ferdinand was world class. He is meant to be a fantastic footballer but today he showed he is a great defender as well."

A defender's job at United requires more than it would at other, less successful clubs. Rio also plays some constructive football, bringing the ball out of defence with grace instead of launching it forward like a Sunday League centre-half. Any defender at any level, even in your local park, could learn a lot from watching him.

Fergie's
FLEXIBLE
DEFENDERS

Brown
Silvestre
O'Shea

40

Wes Brown

Date of birth: **13 October 1979**
Birthplace: **Manchester**
Date signed: **4 November 1996, from United's academy**
United debut: **v Leeds United (Premiership), 4 May 1998**

Wes Brown made a couple of landmark appearances in the 2004/05 season. He made his 100th Premiership start for Manchester United, and his 150th start in all competitions. It was a case of better late than never for the right-back/ centre-back, who has suffered more than his fair share of injuries in the last five or six years. For example, a serious knee problem forced him to sit-out the entire 1999/2000 season. He also missed the first few months of both 2002/03 (broken ankle) and 2003/04 (more knee trouble)!

Not that Wes wants to be pitied, or permitted to play it safe on the football field. Far from it, the tough lad from Longsight in Manchester still gives 100 per cent when challenging for the ball. Just ask Liverpool's lightweight Luis Garcia, who was sent flying when Wes was sent off at Anfield in January 2005.

Brown is often at his bravest in the games against United's big rivals. He was named Man of the Match when the Reds beat Arsenal 1–0 in the 2004 FA Cup semi-final. And at the time of writing this, his only goals for the Reds were scored against Juventus in February 2003 and Newcastle in April 2005. Hopefully there's more to come from Wes in terms of award-winning defensive work and perhaps the odd goal. Like the man himself said, when he signed his new contract in October 2004, "I'm glad I'm going to be here for another four years, so I can show what I can do again."

John O'Shea

Date of birth: **30 April 1981**
Birthplace: **Waterford, Republic of Ireland**
Date signed: **1 August 1998, from United's academy**
United debut: **v Aston Villa (League Cup), 13 October 1999**

John O'Shea is so versatile, he almost ended up on a different page of this book! During the 2004/05 season, the young Irishman played a few games for United in midfield, alongside his international captain Roy Keane. "I really enjoyed centre midfield but first and foremost I still feel I'm a defender," said John, in an interview with the club's match programme. The statistics so far would support that view – most of his appearances have been at left-back, centre-back or right-back. But at the age of 24, there's still time for his position to change again!

John might even fancy his chances as a striker. His height certainly makes him a handful for opposing defenders at free-kicks and corners, and his shooting isn't bad either. He started the Christmas 2004 period with only two goals for United to his name. But by February 2005, he'd increased his tally to five, after scoring against Crystal Palace, Middlesbrough and, wait for it… Arsenal, at Highbury!

Whatever position Fergie asks him to play in, John just wants to be part of the team and to win more medals. In his first full season, 2003/04, he helped

the Reds to win the Premiership title with some excellent performances at left-back. The next year saw him collect an FA Cup winners' medal for the first time, after playing the full 90 minutes of the final against Millwall. In 2004/05, he faced stiff competition for the left-back position from Gabriel Heinze, hence his move into midfield.

Mikael Silvestre

Date of birth: **9 August 1977**
Birthplace: **Chambray-les-Tours, France**
Date signed: **10 September 1999, from Inter Milan**
United debut: **v Liverpool (Premiership), 11 September 1999**

Sir Alex Ferguson signed four players in the season after winning the Treble – but Mikael Silvestre is the only one who has remained a first-team regular. Quinton Fortune has been hampered by injuries and international duties, while the other two - Mark Bosnich and Massimo Taibi – left after failing to impress between the posts.

Silvestre's ability to play in two different positions has helped him to become a key player at Old Trafford. He made his debut as a left-back in 1999 but later switched to the centre to fill the gap left by Jaap Stam's sale, Laurent Blanc's retirement and Wes Brown's injury worries. Mikael admitted in 2005, "I've played as a central defender for the last two seasons and that is where I want to play."

The arrival of Gabriel Heinze from Paris Saint-Germain in the summer of 2004 suggested Silvestre's days of playing on the left flank were well and truly over. His priority now is to nail down his place alongside Ferdinand by fighting off strong competition from the likes of Wes Brown – no easy task!

To do this, Mikael will need to avoid fighting – literally – with opposing players. A skirmish with Swedish international Freddie Ljungberg saw Silvestre achieve an unwanted first on 1 February 2005, against Arsenal – the first red card of his United career. Suspended, he lost his place in the team to Brown for the next four games.

It can be a player's worst nightmare, having a team-mate who's ready, willing and able to replace you when you make a mistake.

But if you ask Sir Alex, he'll tell you it's a manager's dream… being spoilt for choice!

Manchester United have an immensely proud record of bringing young players through the ranks; from the days of Matt Busby's Babes, to Fergie's Fledglings of the early nineties, the Reds have always tried to develop their own talented young players.

Sir Alex Ferguson says: "We give young players a chance, that's the great beauty of this club. Sir Matt Busby started that and I can't ever see it changing."

Here, we look at six promising young Reds hoping to forge a career at Old Trafford…

Giuseppe Rossi
Position: Striker
Date of birth: 1 February 1987
Birthplace: New Jersey, USA
Date signed: 6 July 2004

Giuseppe Rossi was born in the USA but has dual nationality – American and Italian. In fact, he was signed from Parma, in Italy, in July 2004. An intelligent passer and clinical finisher, Rossi quickly set about making an impression during his first season with the Reds. Sir Alex's traditionally youthful approach to the League Cup meant the young forward made his United debut in November 2004 as a late substitute against Crystal Palace. He added a second appearance three weeks later – again as a substitute – against Arsenal in the competition's quarter-final. Rossi was rewarded for his fine performances in the Reserves by being included in United's 25-man Champions League squad for the second half of the season. Ferguson, rarely one to overstate a player's potential, says: "He has a bright future ahead of him. He's probably the coolest player at the club in terms of his play around the penalty box." Praise indeed.

Gerard Pique
Position: Defender
Date of birth: 2 February 1987
Birthplace: Barcelona, Spain
Date signed: 1 July 2004

When a player arrives from a club like Barcelona, you expect him to be a cultured and accomplished player. **Gerard Pique** (pronounced pee-kay) is certainly that. A calm and composed centre-half, Pique wasted little time making his mark at the club. Again, like Rossi, Pique's debut arrived in the Carling Cup, the Catalan defender replacing John O'Shea in the second half of United's 3–0 win over Crewe. Pique made his Champions League debut from the bench in the 3–0 away defeat to Fenerbahce and earned his first start for the club in the 0–0 FA Cup draw with Exeter City in January 2005. Pique has good aerial presence but is equally comfortable with the ball at his feet. His sound reading of the game is evident even at his tender age.

WATCH

Floribert Ngalula
Position: Midfielder
Date of birth: 7 March 1987
Birthplace: Brussels, Belgium
Date signed: 1 July 2003

Floribert Ngalula played as a central defender when he first arrived from Royal Antwerp, but his athleticism has since been put to better use in central midfield. His talent for breaking up opposition attacks were an asset in United's reserve teams as they won both the Pontin's League and the FA Premier Reserve League in 2004/05. But medals and trophies weren't the only things for Floribert Ngalula (pronounced un-ga-loola) to celebrate in his second year. He also signed a professional contract and was given a first-team squad number (41).

Jonny Evans
Position: Defender
Date of birth: 3 January 1987
Birthplace: Belfast, N. Ireland
Date signed: 1 July 2004

Jonny Evans is hoping to follow the same fast track that saw Wes Brown become a household name – from United's youth team to the first team in a few short years. He made a good start to this, making his debut for the reserves when aged only 16. Jonny's achievements off the pitch are also impressive. He was presented with the governor's award for the best exam results at Ashton-on-Mersey School – where United's young players are educated – after gaining nine grade As or A stars in his GCSEs. He has since studied maths at A-level, as well as learning on the field from some of the best players in the beautiful game. A tall and commanding central defender, Evans admits to being influenced by Rio Ferdinand and also Roy Keane, for his drive and winning mentality.

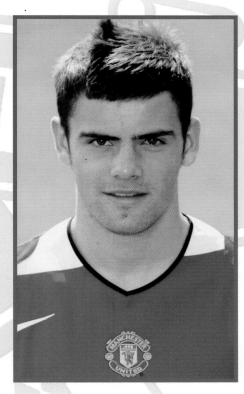

Darron Gibson
Position: Midfielder
Date of birth: 25 October 1987
Birthplace: Derry, N. Ireland
Date signed: 1 July 2004

United first spotted **Darron Gibson** when he attended a training session in Belfast at the age of 12 – but a mix-up meant he was overlooked when other players were called back for further coaching! Fortunately, his talent attracted their attention again when he was 14. An attacking central midfield player, Gibson is blessed with a broad range of passing and a lethal shot. A lifelong United fan, he was set to join Leicester, Leeds or Sunderland before the phone call came from his beloved Reds!

Wayne's World

4

I love training, me. Right, free-kick No. 138…

1

Crikey! Look at the time! Ronaldo, where are all the footballs? We need to start training.

2

I don't know, boss. I haven't even been able to practise any step-overs today.

5

What's this? Wayne, you're using every single football.

3

Hang on a minute, Gaffer. There's one…

Hey, where's Wayne off to? He's got one under his arm.

6

44

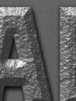

Neville

FORMIDABLE FULL-BACKS

Heinze

Neville

Gary Neville

Date of birth: 18 February 1975
Birthplace: Bury
Date signed: 8 July 1991 (trainee),
2 January 1993 (professional)
United debut: v Torpedo Moscow
(UEFA Cup), September 1992

By the time you read this, Gary Neville could have 500 United appearances under his belt! It's an impressive feat, one which only a handful of players have achieved in the club's illustrious history. Making his debut in the UEFA Cup in 1992, the elder Neville brother has since become United's most experienced player ever in terms of European competition. Of course, he's also played on numerous occasions for England. In fact, there can't be many of the world's top wingers and forwards whom Gary hasn't marked or stopped with a shuddering tackle!

It takes one to know one as far as top players go, and Gary rates three of his longest-serving team-mates as the best in the business. "I think Keane, Scholesy and Giggsy are our best, our most important and most difficult-to-replace players. They've got a class and quality that has been paramount in the success if the last ten years."

If Gary wasn't so modest, he could be talking about himself. He's also been an important player for the Reds in recent years. The right-back first nailed down a regular place in 1994/95 when the team finished second in the league and reached – but lost – the FA Cup Final. In 2004/05, Gary watched from the

bench as United lost the Cup Final again, this time to Arsenal. This cruel blow rounded off a rollercoaster season of personal highs and lows, from scoring against Lyon at Old Trafford to being sent off at Everton. Here's to more goals and less red cards, Gary!

Gabriel Heinze

Date of birth: 19 April 1978
Birthplace: Crespo, Argentina
Date signed: 11 June 2004, from
Paris St Germain
United debut: v Bolton Wanderers
(Premiership), 11 September 2004

Gabriel Heinze's first season as a Manchester United player started spectacularly, with a goal, but ended cruelly, with an injury. The Argentine defender damaged his ankle in the 2-1 win over Newcastle at Old Trafford in April 2005. The reaction of the home fans – standing and applauding as he was stretchered off the field – spoke volumes for the impact that Heinze had in his debut term.

In his debut match, against Bolton, Gabriel scored for the first and only time in 2004/05. But it was his all-round display at the Reebok Stadium which really impressed the travelling Reds fans. Heinze's work-rate, attitude and willingness to fight for the ball made him a worthy addition to United's back-four.

Wearing the number four shirt, Gabriel patrols the area that once belonged to some of the best number threes in the club's history. Like Denis Irwin in the '90s and Arthur Albiston in the '80s, he loves to get forward and join the attack. And who can blame him? Defending can sometimes be a boring job when you play for United!

Gabriel is actually the second player from Argentina to wear the number four shirt for Manchester United. Hopefully, he'll be more successful and more popular than his predecessor Juan Sebastian Veron, who left to join Chelsea after just two seasons at Old Trafford. On that score, it's so far, so good for Gabriel. All he has to do now is add a few more gongs to the gold medal he won with Argentina at the 2004 Olympics.

Phil Neville

Date of birth: 21 January 1977
Birthplace: Bury
Date signed: 5 July 1993 (trainee),
1 June 1994 (professional)
United debut: v Manchester City
(Premiership), 11 February 1995

Phil Neville enjoyed the honour of leading United's first team out of the Old Trafford tunnel in 2005, ten years after he did the same with the apprentices' team. But while Phil has fond memories of lifting the FA Youth Cup in 1995, he might want to forget his first experience as a skipper in the FA Cup… drawing 0-0 with non-league Exeter City! Still, it was an important day for some of United's younger players who were trying to make the grade, just as Phil had done a decade earlier.

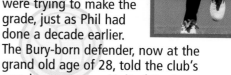

The Bury-born defender, now at the grand old age of 28, told the club's match programme United Review:

"It's a tradition, part of the history of the club, for players from the youth team to progress to the first team. And even though we didn't get the right result against Exeter, the manager shows tremendous faith in the youth players."

Fergie's faith in Phil Neville saw the England international keep his place in the United team for the first six games of 2005, while team-mates and rivals like Fortune, O'Shea, Spector and Silvestre sat on the bench. Of course, he had to return the captain's armband to Roy Keano and he made way eventually for his brother Gary at right-back. But at least he could say he'd played his part in the best defensive period of the season – Phil featured in seven of the eight consecutive games in which the Reds kept a clean sheet, from Boxing Day (26 December) to 22 January. Good work, fella!

Design your own
Away Kit

Here we set you the challenge of designing your very own away kit, in any colour of your choice... except red, of course! To inspire you, we've found photos of six kits that United wore between 2001 and 2005...

Manchester United

enjoyed some brilliant results away from home during 2004/05, not least their league wins at Anfield, Highbury, the Riverside Stadium and Villa Park. One person who enjoys seeing the Reds play at those particular grounds is the person who designs the away kit for Nike, the club's official kit supplier. For it's only in away games against teams like Arsenal, Liverpool, Middlesbrough and Aston Villa that we get to see United's alternative colours — be they white, black, blue or gold.

Centenary Style I
This black and white design — modelled here by Paul Scholes at Villa Park — was one of two kits launched during the 2001/02 season, to mark 100 years since Newton Heath became Manchester United. Look closely and you'll see the trim is gold, the main colour in the other centenary kit.

It's Quite All White
John O'Shea went marching down the wing to great effect in 2002/03, when United won the Premiership title. Here you can see him at Anfield, where the Reds dazzled Dudek in the Liverpool goal with two strikes by Forlan. The December sun shone on O'Shea and his pals all afternoon.

Centenary Style II
Wolves fans might have done a double-take when they saw Roy Keane and Co wearing United's third kit in 2001/02 — it's quite similar to the Molineux club's home colours. Sadly, the gold shirt didn't bring the Reds any luck or silverware. Our photo is from their 3–1 Premiership defeat against Arsenal at Highbury.

In the Navy
Blue is normally associated with another club in Manchester, especially if the shade is sky or laser. But United actually wore an all-blue kit many years ago, even before City won their last trophy! The Reds wore it when they lifted the 1968 European Cup. Twenty-five years later, they wore a similar kit as they outpaced Arsenal in the title race.

Pinstriped at the Park

United won three times at Villa Park in 2004, while wearing the same white shirt with a red horizontal pinstripe. They beat Aston Villa twice – in the FA Cup in January and the Premiership in December. Villa Park also staged the FA Cup semi-final, which United won 1–0 against Arsenal.

Back in Black

Players such as Cantona, Hughes and Kanchelskis looked awesome in black during the Double-winning season of 1993/94. A decade later, the black kit made a welcome return for away matches at Anfield, Highbury and at the Riverside Stadium where David Bellion is captured here, dribbling the ball against Boro.

Nice footwork, Cristiano, but I'm not so sure about the kit!

Get Your Kit On, Cristiano

Once you've decided on a colour scheme and design for your kit, you can use this section of the page to see how it would look on **Cristiano Ronaldo**. Why not photo-copy the picture a few times and try several different designs?

Go on, YOU can do it!

THE

BEST OF ENEMIES

The ten-year battle between **United** and **Arsenal** has been one of the most exciting sagas in the history of English football. Here, we recall five of the best games played between the two great rivals since 1996, the year that **Sir Alex Ferguson** first pitted his wits against **Arsene Wenger**...

FA Cup Semi-Final Replay
Villa Park – 14 April 1999

Arsenal 1   (Bergkamp 69)
Man Utd 2   (Beckham 17, Giggs 109)

Not just one of United's greatest-ever games against Arsenal... probably one of their greatest-ever, full stop! After winning the League and FA Cup Double in his second season, Arsene Wenger was aiming to repeat the feat in his third campaign as Gunners' boss. United were also in the hunt for the two biggest trophies in England, plus the European Cup. Something had to give and sure enough it did. A penalty save by Peter Schmeichel in the last minute and a remarkable solo goal by Ryan Giggs in extra-time won the tie for United at the second time of asking. This epic victory, at the neutral venue of Villa Park, set the Reds en route to the glorious Treble.

Giggs scores his best-ever goal to win an epic tie for United.

Premiership
Highbury – 16 April 2003

Arsenal 2   (Henry 51, 62)
Man Utd 2   (van Nistelrooy 24, Giggs 63)

Fresh from heading north to thrash Newcastle 6–2, the Reds travelled south to tackle Arsenal on a warm April night. Wearing all blue, the Reds drew first blood when van Nistelrooy burst through on the left and fired into the net nearest Arsenal's hardcore fans. The next two goals were also scored at the North Bank end, both by Henry. If Thierry was offside for the second one, then justice was swiftly done. Almost immediately from the restart, Giggs headed in the equaliser. The important action didn't end there – Campbell was later sent off for striking Solskjaer. The suspended centre-back was sorely missed as Arsenal's title bid crumbled in the closing weeks, much to United's delight!

Ruud leaves Cole and Campbell trailing behind at Highbury.

FA Cup Semi-Final
Villa Park – 3 April 2004

Arsenal 0
Man Utd 1   (Scholes 32)

Even the most ardent Reds fan had to admit, Arsenal looked awesome for most of 2003/04 – after all, they didn't lose a single league game! But this was one of the rare occasions when the Gunners looked vulnerable, mainly because United were desperate to stop them winning the same Treble that Fergie had achieved in 1999. Scholes scored the all-important goal but there were many other heroes in United's white, away shirts. To name just three: the dazzling Ronaldo, the determined Darren Fletcher and the dependable Roy Carroll, who made a vital save to deny Dennis Bergkamp when the score was 0–0 in the opening minutes. The Reds went on to win the FA Cup of course; Arsenal, meanwhile, lost their Champions League quarter-final to Chelsea but deservedly won the title.

Fletcher stands his ground against Arsenal goalkeeper Jens Lehmann.

Premiership
Old Trafford – 24 October 2004

Man Utd 2 (van Nistelrooy pen 73, Rooney 90)
Arsenal 0

This meeting will be remembered in the media as the Battle of the Buffet, following a food fight between players after the match! But it was also the game which wrecked Arsenal's unbeaten run in the Premiership, one short of a half-century. Stand-in skipper Ferdinand performed brilliantly to keep Henry at bay but his England colleague Campbell… well, he had a mare! The Arsenal star was found guilty of tripping Rooney and Ruud scored the resulting penalty, just over a year after missing one against the same rivals! Rooney then killed the game with a second goal, as the home fans roared their approval above the din of the driving rain.

Van Nistelrooy celebrates after slotting home the spot-kick.

Premiership
Highbury – 1 February 2005

Arsenal 2 (Vieira 8, Bergkamp 36)
Man Utd 4 (Giggs 18, Ronaldo 54, 58, O'Shea 89)

The great rivals produced some wonderful football in this Tuesday night treat, described by Sir Alex Ferguson as "probably the best Premiership match ever"! Players like Bergkamp and Giggs, both of whom scored in the first half, were inspirational. Arsenal netted first through Vieira and went in at half-time with their noses still in front. At full-time, however, the Gunners had their tails between their legs. The Reds ripped them apart in the second half, especially Ronaldo with his two goals in the space of four minutes. And when O'Shea floated in the fourth, it capped an unforgettable night for the travelling Reds fans and the like-minded millions watching on TV. Not even Silvestre's sending-off could spoil it.

Pires looks dejected, but Brown and O'Shea are delighted.

United Scorers

v Arsenal (1996-2005*)

Only one player has scored a hat-trick for the Reds against Arsenal in the past decade… and he did it in only the first quarter of the match! Dwight Yorke netted in the 3rd, 18th and 22nd minutes of an amazing 6–1 win for United at Old Trafford on 25 February 2001. Keane and Solskjaer also scored in the first half, to make it 5–1 at the break – Henry had equalised for Arsenal between Yorke's first and second goals. Almost the entire second half then passed before Sheringham scored the sixth.

Teddy Sheringham	4
Roy Keane	3
Ryan Giggs	3
Paul Scholes	3
Dwight Yorke	3
David Beckham	2
Andy Cole	2
Cristiano Ronaldo	2
Ole Gunnar Solskjaer	2
Ruud van Nistelrooy	2
David Bellion	1
John O'Shea	1
Wayne Rooney	1
Louis Saha	1
Mikael Silvestre	1
Alan Smith	1
Juan Sebastian Veron	1
Nigel Winterburn (own-goal)	1

List of scorers compiled before 2005 FA Cup Final
*all competitions, including Community Shield

Can you clinch the Premiership?

Manchester United know everything there is to know about winning the Premiership, having done it eight times since 1992. But how much do you know about Manchester United?

Answer most of our United questions correctly and you could gain enough points to finish above Chelsea and reclaim the title from them – see the final 2004/05 table opposite.

There are 38 games in a Premiership season, so we've set 38 questions. A correct answer is classed as a win, so award yourself three points. An incorrect answer is regarded as a loss, which means nil points. If you're stuck for an answer, you're allowed to pass or ignore the question. We'll call this a draw and give you one point, but note – you can only have five draws during the entire quiz.

Best of luck, and may the best team win the Premiership!

1. Manchester United was founded in 1878, but under what name?

2. How many times have Manchester United won the Football League Cup (currently known as the Carling Cup)?

3. Sir Alex Ferguson celebrated his 1,000th game in charge of Manchester United in November 2004. Who did they play against?

4. Roy Keane joined United in 1993 for what was then a British record fee of £3.75m. Which club did the Reds sign him from?

5. Who wore the No.5 shirt for United in the 2005 FA Cup Final?

6. Against which Premiership team did Cristiano Ronaldo make his United debut in August 2003?

7. Who were the opponents during Sir Alex Ferguson's first game in charge at the club?

8. When United won the league for the first time in 26 years, in 1992/93, their two centre-backs started every single game. Can you name them?

9. Ruud van Nistelrooy's best goals tally in a season came in 2002/03. How many did he score?

10. Who holds the club record for most goals scored in a season?

11. Ryan Giggs, Gary Neville, Paul Scholes, Roy Keane – why is Roy Keane the odd one out?

12. Who was Manchester United manager before Sir Alex Ferguson?

13. In what year did Sir Matt Busby guide United to the club's first European Cup?

14. Eric Cantona, Rio Ferdinand and Alan Smith were all signed from which club?

15. The only two British players to have won the World Cup with their country and the European Cup with their club both played for United. Who are they?

16. Carlos Queiroz left Manchester United for one season – 2003/04 – to manage a team in La Liga. Which Spanish club did he take charge of?

17. What is Quinton Fortune's nationality?

18. Wayne Rooney made an instant impact on his United debut in Europe. Against which team did he score a hat-trick?

19. Teddy Sheringham and Ole Gunnar Solskjaer were United's 'super subs' in the European Cup final in 1999, but who did they replace at the Nou Camp?

20. Which player holds the record for most United appearances?

21. Which former player celebrated his 19th birthday on the day United won the European Cup in 1968 by scoring the third goal in the 4–1 win, and was Sir Alex Ferguson's assistant manager in the 1990s?

22. On 11th March 1941, Old Trafford was hit by two German bombs, which seriously damaged the stadium. Where did United play their 'home' games while the stadium was rebuilt?

23. In 2004/05, Ruud van Nistelrooy broke Denis Law's United goal-scoring record in the European Cup. How many goals did Law score in Europe?

24. Darren Fletcher made his United debut in the Champions League in 2003 – against which team?

25. How many England caps did Paul Scholes earn before he retired from international duty after the 2004 European Championships?

26. Cristiano Ronaldo was signed from which Portuguese club?

27. In which city was Ryan Giggs born?

28. Promising young Reds striker Giuseppe Rossi holds an Italian passport, but where in America was he born?

29. United signed exciting defensive prospect Gerard Pique from which top Spanish side?

30. Who has made the most substitute appearances in Manchester United's history?

31. Who was the first Brazilian ever to play for United?

32. Louis Saha and David Bellion were both born in which French city?

33. Cristiano Ronaldo, Darren Fletcher and Wayne Rooney – who is the youngest?

34. On what date does Wayne Rooney celebrate his birthday?

35. Who is Manchester United's assistant manager?

36. Who were United's opponents in the 2005 FA Cup final?

37. Who wears the No.4 shirt for Manchester United?

38. Which non-league team forced United to a replay in the FA Cup third round in 2004/05?

ANSWERS ON PAGE 60

Final League Table 2004/05		
Team	P	Pts
Chelsea	38	95
Arsenal	38	83
Manchester United	38	77
Everton	38	61
Liverpool	38	58
Bolton Wanderers	38	58
Middlesbrough	38	55
Manchester City	38	52
Tottenham Hotspur	38	52
Aston Villa	38	47
Charlton Athletic	38	46
Birmingham City	38	45
Fulham	38	44
Newcastle United	38	44
Blackburn Rovers	38	42
Portsmouth	38	39
West Bromwich	38	34
Crystal Palace	38	33
Norwich City	38	33
Southampton	38	32

Commentary QUIZ

Sometimes special moments in football – especially goals – are forever associated with the words of a TV commentator. For example, who could ever forget what ITV's Clive Tyldesley said, just before United equalised in the 1999 European Cup Final. "Can United score? They always score..."

Here, we present six extracts of TV commentary from the 2004/05 season – each one describes a goal scored by United. All you have to do is match the words in A to F with the photos numbered 1 to 6. The answers are on page 60.

1

Commentary B

"Here's Fletcher... Scholes... on to Gary Neville. Couple of minutes of stoppage time being played. Wayne Rooney... here's Keane, clever little reverse ball for Giggs. Queuing up for the cross... Scorer!"

Commentary A

"Gary Neville with a diagonal... Giggs keeping it alive for Manchester United, the volley from Scorer! Oh, what an absolutely stunning goal from Goal Scorer, in the colours of Manchester United! No wonder the man who signed him is smiling."

Commentary C
"Ronaldo's now gone into the middle. As he showed at Euro 2004, he can be quite useful in the air as well. It's Giggs who swings it in... and coming round the back was Goal Scorer! And Manchester United are ahead! The man who rejected Liverpool has scored against them!"

Commentary D
"Couple of minutes of the first half remaining. Giggs swings it in and Silvestre's header... and Scorer has scored on his Manchester United debut! What a way to announce your arrival in English football!"

Commentary E
"Now then, Scorer... almost invited to shoot, he does and scores! Mistake by the goalkeeper, it went right through him and Goal Scorer has given Manchester United the lead!"

Commentary F
"Interesting moves down there on the touchline but United are going to come back and retake the free-kick. Scholes... is this the final attack for Manchester United? Louis Saha... Scorer! Unbelievable!"

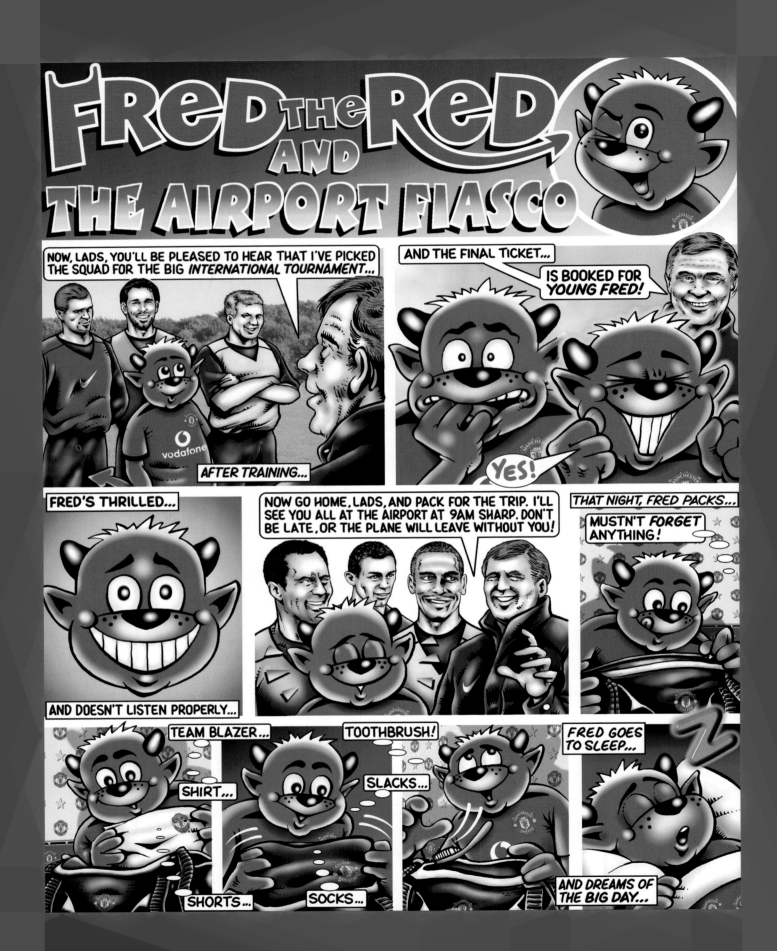

Answers to Puzzles

Who Am I?
pages 34–35

(Reading from top to bottom, then left to right)

1. Gabriel Heinze
2. Alan Smith
3. Mikael Silvestre
4. Cristiano Ronaldo
5. Darren Fletcher
6. Wayne Rooney

Can You Do an Ole?
pages 36–37

1. Ole Gunnar Solskjaer
2. David Beckham
3. Andy Cole
4. David Beckham
5. Ole Gunnar Solskjaer

Can You Clinch the Premiership?
pages 54–55

1. Newton Heath LYR (Lancashire and Yorkshire Railway)
2. Once
3. Olympique Lyonnais (Lyon)
4. Nottingham Forest
5. Rio Ferdinand
6. Bolton Wanderers, as a second-half substitute
7. Oxford United (Manchester United lost 2–0)
8. Gary Pallister and Steve Bruce
9. 44
10. Denis Law (46)
11. Giggs, Neville and Scholes all came through the club's acclaimed youth system
12. Ron Atkinson (lost his job after poor form in the 1986/87 season)
13. 1968 – United beat Benfica 4–1 in the final at Wembley on 29 May
14. Leeds United
15. Nobby Stiles and Sir Bobby Charlton
16. Real Madrid
17. South African
18. Fenerbahce
19. Jesper Blomqvist (Sheringham), Andy Cole (Solskjaer)
20. Sir Bobby Charlton (752 appearances)
21. Brian Kidd
22. Maine Road (Manchester City's old stadium)
23. 28
24. FC Basel
25. 68 caps
26. Sporting Lisbon
27. Cardiff
28. New Jersey
29. Barcelona
30. Ole Gunnar Solskjaer
31. Kleberson
32. Paris
33. Wayne Rooney
34. 24 October
35. Carlos Queiroz
36. Arsenal
37. Gabriel Heinze
38. Exeter City

Commentary Quiz
pages 56–57

A. 5 – Alan Smith v Norwich City (Home)
B. 4 – John O'Shea v Crystal Palace (Home)
C. 6 – Mikael Silvestre v Liverpool (Home)
D. 1 – Gabriel Heinze v Bolton Wanderers (Away)
E. 3 – Wayne Rooney v Liverpool (Away)
F. 2 – Alan Smith v Blackburn Rovers (Away)